LOOK INSIDE
CROSS-SECTIONS
SPACE

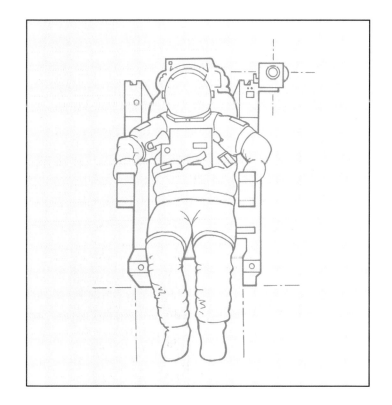

LOOK INSIDE
CROSS-SECTIONS
SPACE

ILLUSTRATED BY

NICK LIPSCOMBE AND GARY BIGGIN

WRITTEN BY

MOIRA BUTTERFIELD

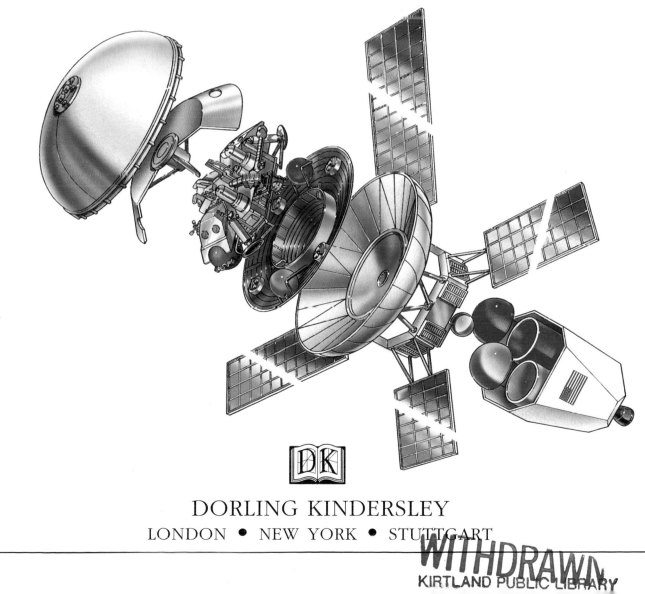

DK

DORLING KINDERSLEY
LONDON • NEW YORK • STUTTGART

A DORLING KINDERSLEY BOOK

Art Editor Dorian Spencer Davies
Designers Sharon Grant, Sara Hill
Senior Art Editor C. David Gillingwater
Project Editor Constance Novis
Senior Editor John C. Miles
U.S. Assistant Editor Camela Decaire
Production Louise Barratt
Consultant Robin Kerrod

First American edition, 1994
2 4 6 8 10 9 7 5 3 1
Published in the United States
by Dorling Kindersley Publishing, Inc.,
95 Madison Avenue, New York, New York 10016

Library of Congress Cataloging - in - Publication Data

Butterfield, Moira, 1961-
Space / written by Moira Butterfield;
illustrated by Gary Biggin and Nick Lipscombe. – 1st American ed.
p. cm. – (Look inside cross-sections)
Includes index.
ISBN 1-56458-682-0
1. Astronautics – Juvenile literature.
[1. Astronautics.]
I. Biggin, Gary, ill.
II. Lipscombe, Nick, ill. III. Title. IV. Series.
TL793. B86 1994
629. 47 – dc20   94 – 18480
                                    CIP
                                    AC

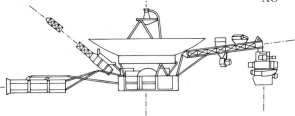

Reproduced by Dot Gradations, Essex
Printed and bound by Proost, Belgium

CONTENTS

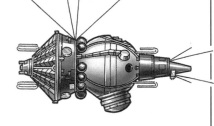

MERCURY/VOSKHOD 2

SATURN V

APOLLO LM

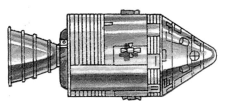

APOLLO CSM

SKYLAB

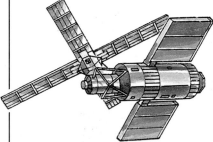

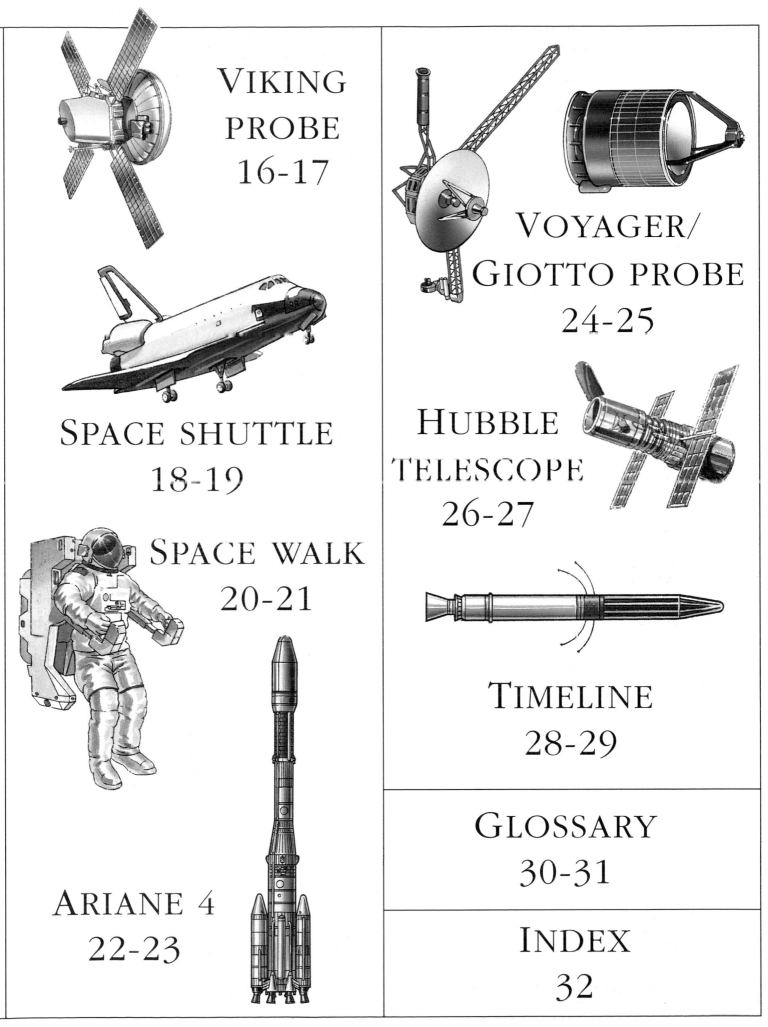

MERCURY

ON OCTOBER 4, 1957, THE USSR launched the world's first satellite, called *Sputnik 1*. As this small aluminum sphere hurtled through space, it set off what was to be known as the "Space Race," with scientists in the USSR and the US competing to achieve supremacy in space. On February 20, 1962, the Americans put their first astronaut ("star sailor") into orbit in the Mercury spacecraft *Friendship 7*. His name was John Glenn and he became a national hero after he orbited the Earth three times in a trip lasting five hours.

Aerodynamic spike

Escape rocket

Rescue rockets
The cone-shaped capsule had a rescue tower on top with an extra rocket. These could be used to separate the craft from the main rocket if something went wrong during the launch.

Tower separation rocket

Infrared horizon sensor

Conical ribbon drogue parachute

Hydrogen peroxide bottle

Pitch thruster

Yaw thruster

Main and reserve ring-sail parachutes

Aerodynamic fairing

Liftoff
A spacecraft must blast off at high speed or it will be pulled back to the Earth by gravity. *Friendship* was launched on top of a big rocket. Once the rocket had boosted it up, the manned capsule separated away and the rocket fell back toward the Earth.

Under pressure
Around the Earth there is a layer of air called the atmosphere that pushes down on us. We need this pressure; without it, our lungs wouldn't work. Out in space, pressure has to be provided artificially. John Glenn's capsule was pressurized using pure oxygen.

Instrument panel

Skin shingles

Double-walled pressurized cabin

Abort control

That floating feeling
Out in space people and objects float unless they are secured to something. Glenn was one of the first people to experience the feeling, and he liked it. But other astronauts have suffered from space sickness, which feels like being carsick.

Manual flight control

Form-fitting couch and restraints

Heat shield

Hot and fast
A spacecraft returns to the Earth at very high speeds. On reentering the atmosphere, heat shields on the outside glow white-hot, but stop the heat from passing inside the capsule.

Retro-rocket

Separation rocket

Roll thruster

TECHNICAL DATA

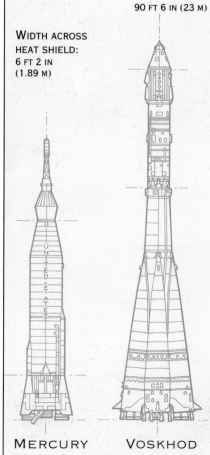

HEIGHT (INCLUDING TOWER):
26 FT (7.9 M)

HEIGHT (INCLUDING SPACECRAFT):
125 FT 10 IN (38.4 M)

DIAMETER:
90 FT 6 IN (23 M)

WIDTH ACROSS HEAT SHIELD:
6 FT 2 IN (1.89 M)

MERCURY   VOSKHOD

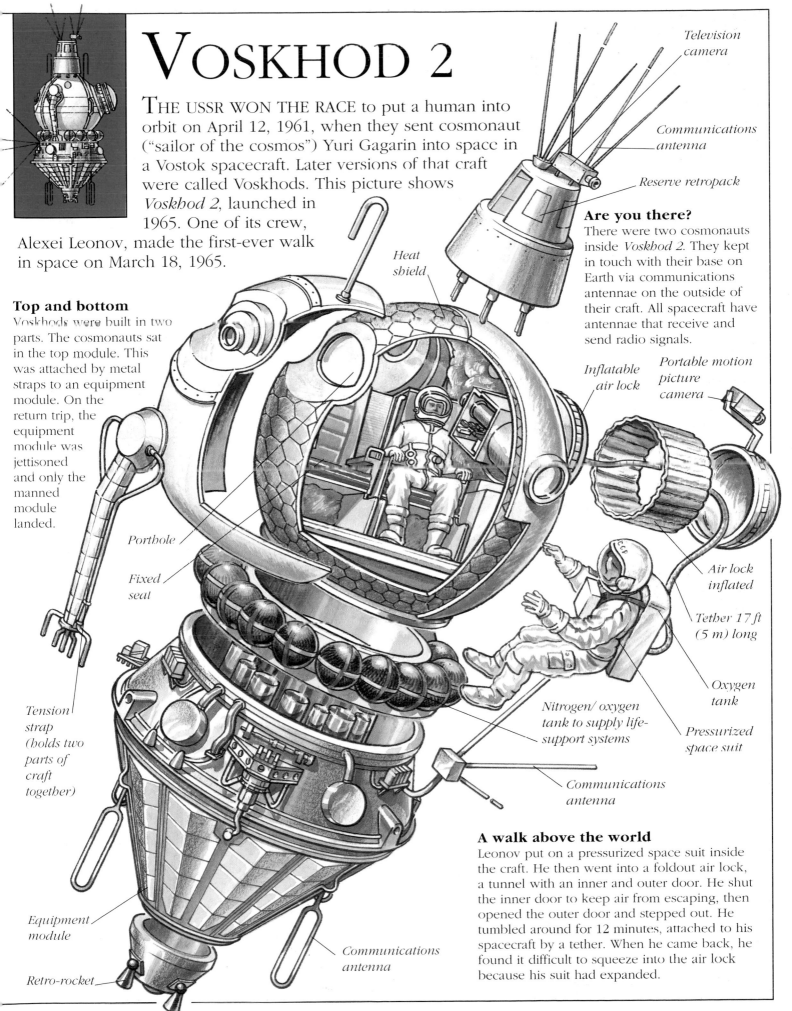

VOSKHOD 2

THE USSR WON THE RACE to put a human into orbit on April 12, 1961, when they sent cosmonaut ("sailor of the cosmos") Yuri Gagarin into space in a Vostok spacecraft. Later versions of that craft were called Voskhods. This picture shows *Voskhod 2*, launched in 1965. One of its crew, Alexei Leonov, made the first-ever walk in space on March 18, 1965.

Top and bottom

Voskhods were built in two parts. The cosmonauts sat in the top module. This was attached by metal straps to an equipment module. On the return trip, the equipment module was jettisoned and only the manned module landed.

Television camera

Communications antenna

Reserve retropack

Heat shield

Are you there?

There were two cosmonauts inside *Voskhod 2*. They kept in touch with their base on Earth via communications antennae on the outside of their craft. All spacecraft have antennae that receive and send radio signals.

Inflatable air lock

Portable motion picture camera

Porthole

Fixed seat

Air lock inflated

Tether 17 ft (5 m) long

Oxygen tank

Tension strap (holds two parts of craft together)

Nitrogen/ oxygen tank to supply life-support systems

Pressurized space suit

Communications antenna

A walk above the world

Leonov put on a pressurized space suit inside the craft. He then went into a foldout air lock, a tunnel with an inner and outer door. He shut the inner door to keep air from escaping, then opened the outer door and stepped out. He tumbled around for 12 minutes, attached to his spacecraft by a tether. When he came back, he found it difficult to squeeze into the air lock because his suit had expanded.

Equipment module

Communications antenna

Retro-rocket

SATURN V

"FIVE, FOUR, THREE, TWO, ONE — We have liftoff!" At the end of a launchpad countdown like this, the roar of giant engines fills the sky and huge engine nozzles spit columns of white-hot flames and gas, pushing an entire rocket upward. Between 1968 and 1972, giant *Saturn V* rockets carried the American Apollo manned missions toward the Moon. The noise of a Saturn launch sounded like a volcano erupting. A *Saturn V* took *Apollo 11* into space on July 16, 1969. Four days later, two of the crew members made history when they became the first humans to walk on the Moon.

Inside the engines
Inside a rocket there are separate tanks of liquid fuel and liquid oxygen, powerful propellants. They are pumped into a combustion chamber inside each engine. There they are mixed and set on fire, producing the hot gases needed to propel the rocket.

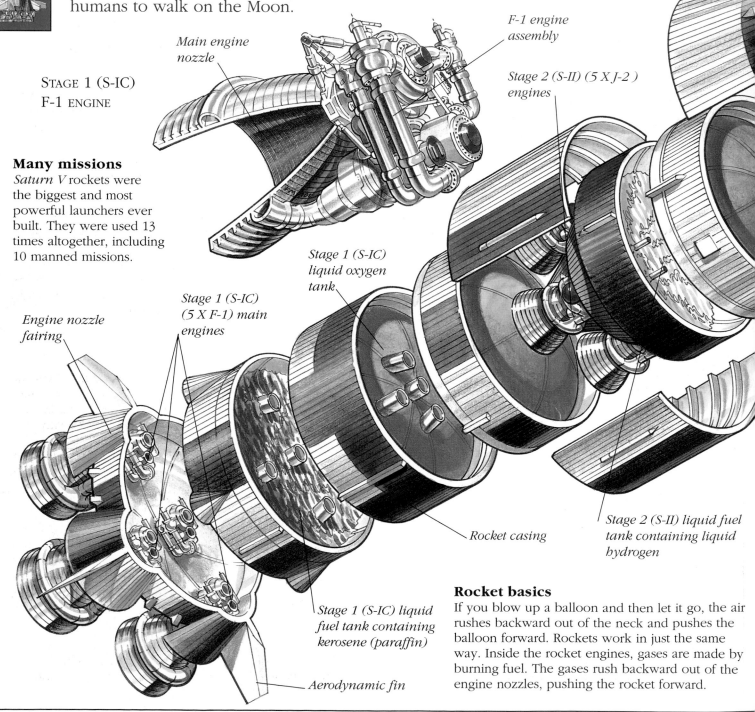

STAGE 1 (S-IC)
F-1 ENGINE

Main engine nozzle

F-1 engine assembly

Stage 2 (S-II) (5 X J-2) engines

Many missions
Saturn V rockets were the biggest and most powerful launchers ever built. They were used 13 times altogether, including 10 manned missions.

Stage 1 (S-IC) liquid oxygen tank

Engine nozzle fairing

Stage 1 (S-IC) (5 X F-1) main engines

Rocket casing

Stage 2 (S-II) liquid fuel tank containing liquid hydrogen

Stage 1 (S-IC) liquid fuel tank containing kerosene (paraffin)

Aerodynamic fin

Rocket basics
If you blow up a balloon and then let it go, the air rushes backward out of the neck and pushes the balloon forward. Rockets work in just the same way. Inside the rocket engines, gases are made by burning fuel. The gases rush backward out of the engine nozzles, pushing the rocket forward.

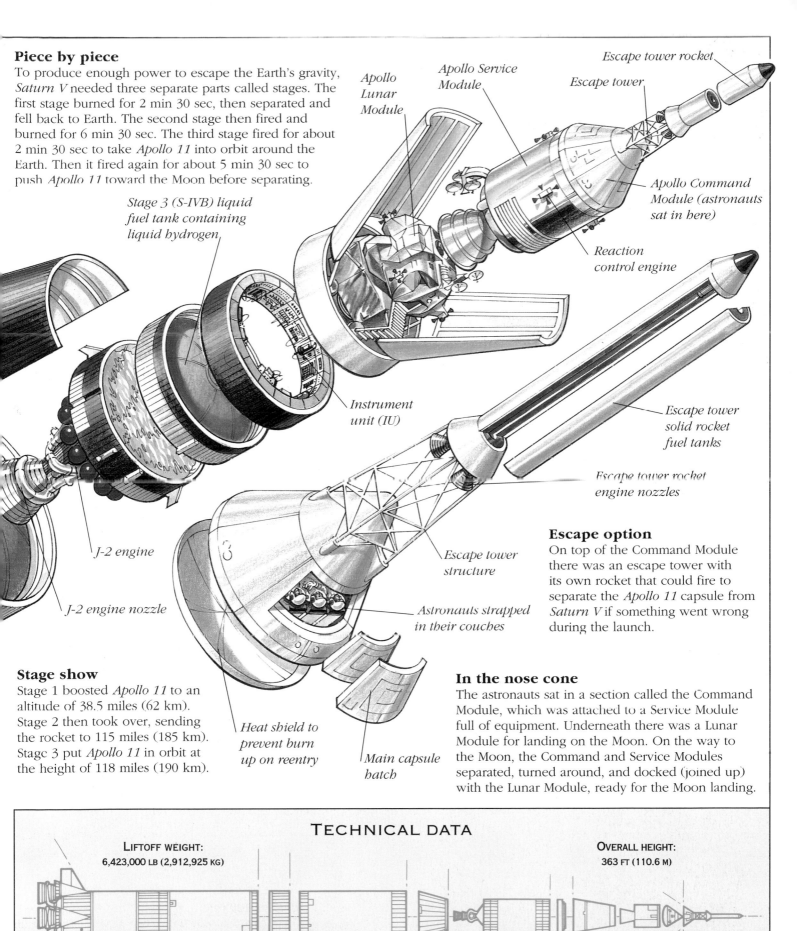

Piece by piece

To produce enough power to escape the Earth's gravity, *Saturn V* needed three separate parts called stages. The first stage burned for 2 min 30 sec, then separated and fell back to Earth. The second stage then fired and burned for 6 min 30 sec. The third stage fired for about 2 min 30 sec to take *Apollo 11* into orbit around the Earth. Then it fired again for about 5 min 30 sec to push *Apollo 11* toward the Moon before separating.

Stage 3 (S-IVB) liquid fuel tank containing liquid hydrogen

Apollo Lunar Module

Apollo Service Module

Escape tower rocket

Escape tower

Apollo Command Module (astronauts sat in here)

Reaction control engine

Instrument unit (IU)

J-2 engine

J-2 engine nozzle

Escape tower solid rocket fuel tanks

Escape tower rocket engine nozzles

Escape tower structure

Astronauts strapped in their couches

Heat shield to prevent burn up on reentry

Main capsule hatch

Escape option

On top of the Command Module there was an escape tower with its own rocket that could fire to separate the *Apollo 11* capsule from *Saturn V* if something went wrong during the launch.

Stage show

Stage 1 boosted *Apollo 11* to an altitude of 38.5 miles (62 km). Stage 2 then took over, sending the rocket to 115 miles (185 km). Stage 3 put *Apollo 11* in orbit at the height of 118 miles (190 km).

In the nose cone

The astronauts sat in a section called the Command Module, which was attached to a Service Module full of equipment. Underneath there was a Lunar Module for landing on the Moon. On the way to the Moon, the Command and Service Modules separated, turned around, and docked (joined up) with the Lunar Module, ready for the Moon landing.

TECHNICAL DATA

LIFTOFF WEIGHT:
6,423,000 LB (2,912,925 KG)

OVERALL HEIGHT:
363 FT (110.6 M)

F-1 ENGINE NOZZLE:
19 FT (5.79 M) TALL, 12 FT 6 IN (3.81 M) WIDE

STAGE 1 LENGTH:
137 FT 8 IN (42 M)

ESCAPE TOWER:
33 FT 5 IN (10.2 M) LONG

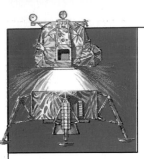

APOLLO LM

NASA HAD LAUNCHED A SERIES OF manned Apollo test flights, gradually taking astronauts closer to the Moon. Finally, on *Apollo 11*, astronauts were ready to land on the Moon's surface!

As *Apollo 11* went into lunar orbit, two members of the crew, Edwin "Buzz" Aldrin and Neil Armstrong, crawled into the Lunar Module (LM for short). The module, code-named "Eagle," separated from the Command and Service Module and dropped down to the Moon, using rockets and radar to guide it. The astronauts depressurized the cabin and checked their equipment. Then, on July 20, 1969, Armstrong opened a hatch, left the module, and took the first step on the Moon's surface.

Space bug
The Lunar Module had a strange insectlike shape. But because it operated only in space, where there is no air, its designers didn't need to worry about giving it a streamlined shape.

Reaction control system fuel

Reaction control system oxidizer

VHF antenna

Docking hatch

Relay box

Ascent fuel tank

Reaction control system pressurant

Ascent engine

Portable life-support system

Entry/Exit platform and rails

Entry hatch

Rendezvous radar

Steerable antenna

Pilot's console

Reaction control system thruster

Room inside
Inside the pressurized cabin there were computer consoles, viewing windows, and supplies. When the crew went out, they had to carefully monitor the controls of their bulky space suits. If they ran out of oxygen, water, or any other supply, they would see warning lights and return to the cabin. The *Apollo 11* astronauts spent 2 1/2 hours on the surface of the Moon before returning to the LM cabin.

Taking off again
The "descent stage," the bottom section with the legs, served as a launchpad for the "ascent stage" when it was time to leave the Moon. It was left on the surface as the ascent stage flew up to dock with the Command and Service Modules. Once the crew were safely back in the Command Module, the ascent stage was also jettisoned.

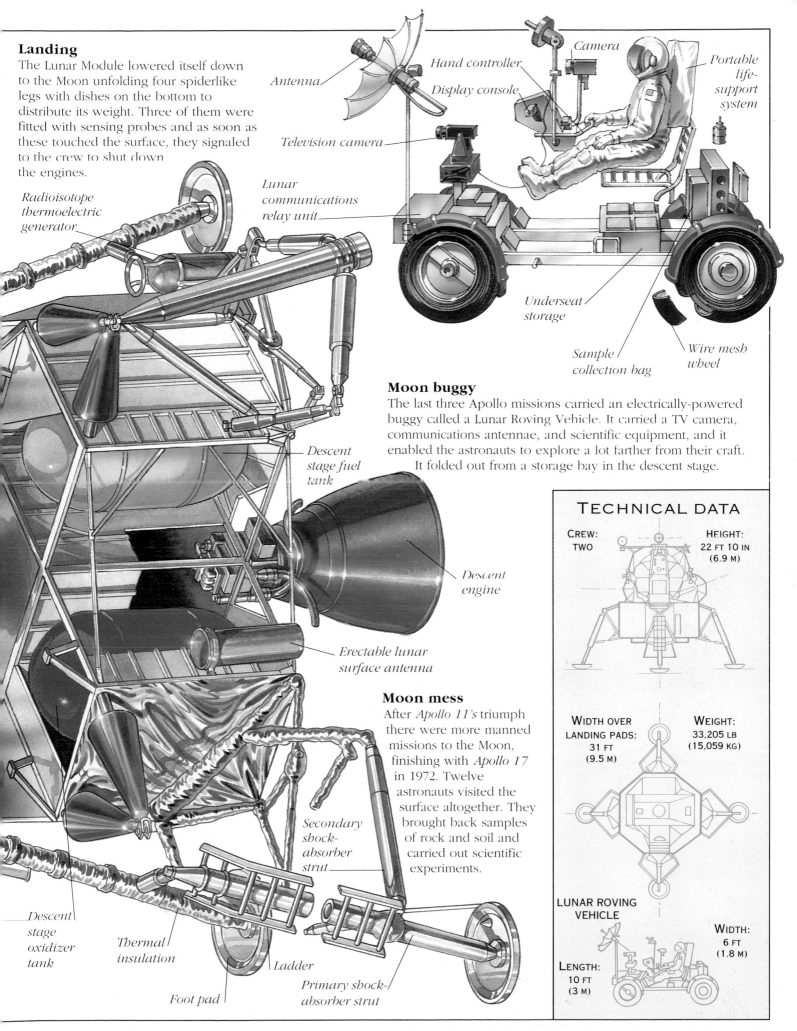

Landing

The Lunar Module lowered itself down to the Moon unfolding four spiderlike legs with dishes on the bottom to distribute its weight. Three of them were fitted with sensing probes and as soon as these touched the surface, they signaled to the crew to shut down the engines.

Antenna

Hand controller

Camera

Display console

Portable life-support system

Radioisotope thermoelectric generator

Lunar communications relay unit

Television camera

Underseat storage

Sample collection bag

Wire mesh wheel

Moon buggy

The last three Apollo missions carried an electrically-powered buggy called a Lunar Roving Vehicle. It carried a TV camera, communications antennae, and scientific equipment, and it enabled the astronauts to explore a lot farther from their craft. It folded out from a storage bay in the descent stage.

Descent stage fuel tank

Descent engine

Erectable lunar surface antenna

Moon mess

After *Apollo 11's* triumph there were more manned missions to the Moon, finishing with *Apollo 17* in 1972. Twelve astronauts visited the surface altogether. They brought back samples of rock and soil and carried out scientific experiments.

Secondary shock-absorber strut

Descent stage oxidizer tank

Thermal insulation

Ladder

Foot pad

Primary shock-absorber strut

TECHNICAL DATA

CREW: TWO

HEIGHT: 22 FT 10 IN (6.9 M)

WIDTH OVER LANDING PADS: 31 FT (9.5 M)

WEIGHT: 33,205 LB (15,059 KG)

LUNAR ROVING VEHICLE

LENGTH: 10 FT (3 M)

WIDTH: 6 FT (1.8 M)

APOLLO CSM

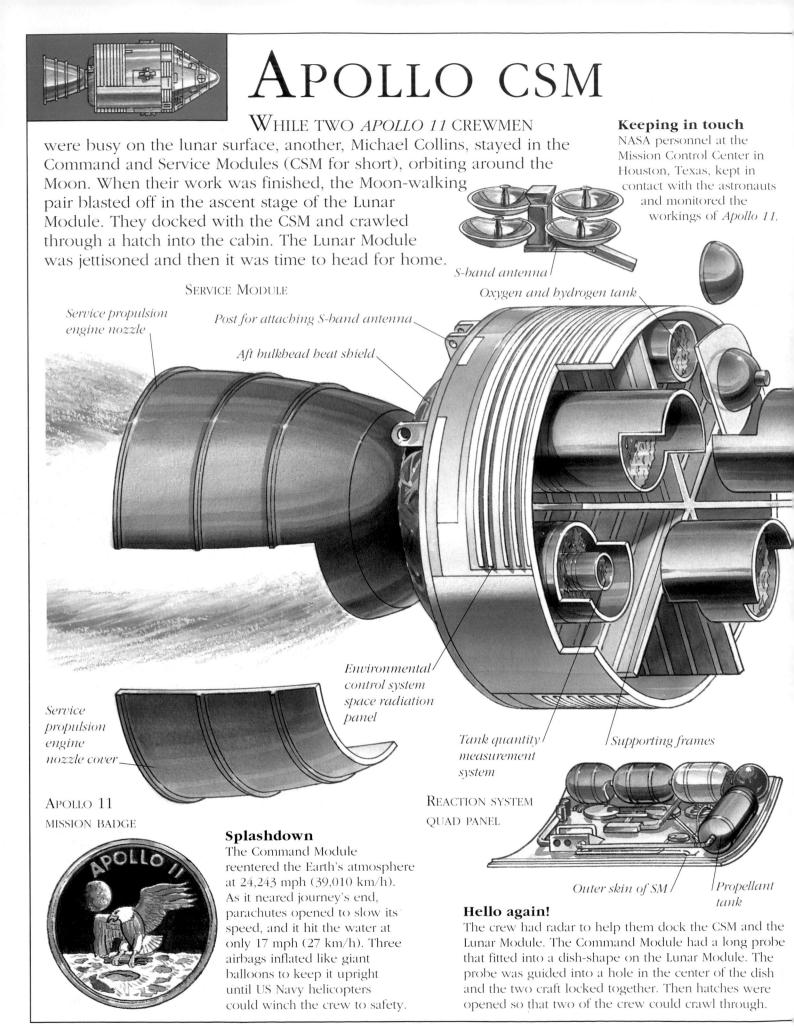

WHILE TWO *APOLLO 11* CREWMEN were busy on the lunar surface, another, Michael Collins, stayed in the Command and Service Modules (CSM for short), orbiting around the Moon. When their work was finished, the Moon-walking pair blasted off in the ascent stage of the Lunar Module. They docked with the CSM and crawled through a hatch into the cabin. The Lunar Module was jettisoned and then it was time to head for home.

Keeping in touch
NASA personnel at the Mission Control Center in Houston, Texas, kept in contact with the astronauts and monitored the workings of *Apollo 11*.

S-band antenna

SERVICE MODULE

Service propulsion engine nozzle

Post for attaching S-band antenna

Aft bulkhead heat shield

Oxygen and hydrogen tank

Environmental control system space radiation panel

Tank quantity measurement system

Supporting frames

Service propulsion engine nozzle cover

APOLLO 11
MISSION BADGE

REACTION SYSTEM
QUAD PANEL

Outer skin of SM

Propellant tank

Splashdown
The Command Module reentered the Earth's atmosphere at 24,243 mph (39,010 km/h). As it neared journey's end, parachutes opened to slow its speed, and it hit the water at only 17 mph (27 km/h). Three airbags inflated like giant balloons to keep it upright until US Navy helicopters could winch the crew to safety.

Hello again!
The crew had radar to help them dock the CSM and the Lunar Module. The Command Module had a long probe that fitted into a dish-shape on the Lunar Module. The probe was guided into a hole in the center of the dish and the two craft locked together. Then hatches were opened so that two of the crew could crawl through.

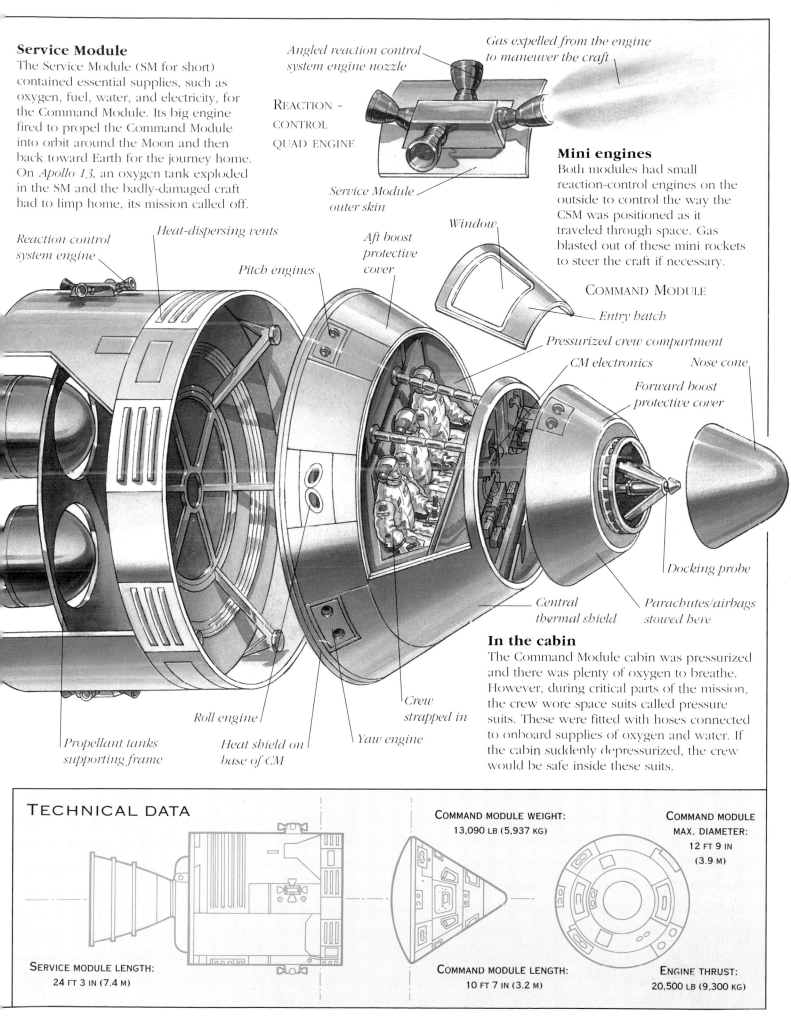

Service Module

The Service Module (SM for short) contained essential supplies, such as oxygen, fuel, water, and electricity, for the Command Module. Its big engine fired to propel the Command Module into orbit around the Moon and then back toward Earth for the journey home. On *Apollo 13*, an oxygen tank exploded in the SM and the badly-damaged craft had to limp home, its mission called off.

Angled reaction control system engine nozzle

Gas expelled from the engine to maneuver the craft

REACTION - CONTROL QUAD ENGINE

Service Module outer skin

Mini engines

Both modules had small reaction-control engines on the outside to control the way the CSM was positioned as it traveled through space. Gas blasted out of these mini rockets to steer the craft if necessary.

COMMAND MODULE

Reaction control system engine

Heat-dispersing vents

Pitch engines

Aft boost protective cover

Window

Entry hatch

Pressurized crew compartment

CM electronics

Nose cone

Forward boost protective cover

Docking probe

Central thermal shield

Parachutes/airbags stowed here

Propellant tanks supporting frame

Roll engine

Heat shield on base of CM

Crew strapped in

Yaw engine

In the cabin

The Command Module cabin was pressurized and there was plenty of oxygen to breathe. However, during critical parts of the mission, the crew wore space suits called pressure suits. These were fitted with hoses connected to onboard supplies of oxygen and water. If the cabin suddenly depressurized, the crew would be safe inside these suits.

TECHNICAL DATA

SERVICE MODULE LENGTH: 24 FT 3 IN (7.4 M)

COMMAND MODULE WEIGHT: 13,090 LB (5,937 KG)

COMMAND MODULE MAX. DIAMETER: 12 FT 9 IN (3.9 M)

COMMAND MODULE LENGTH: 10 FT 7 IN (3.2 M)

ENGINE THRUST: 20,500 LB (9,300 KG)

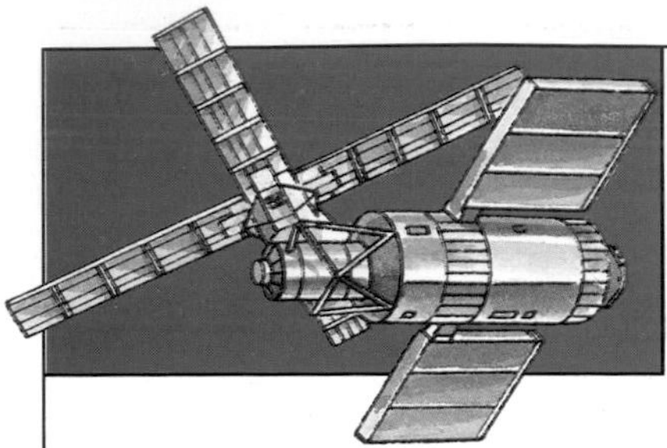

SKYLAB

ONCE THE US HAD LANDED HUMANS on the Moon, the next step was to build a space station where people could live and work. The Russians launched a space station called *Salyut I* in 1971. The Americans launched *Skylab*, shown below, in 1973. During 1973 and 1974, it was home to three different astronaut crews, who traveled to it in Apollo spacecraft. Their bodies were constantly monitored to see how well they coped with long-term life in space. They spent their time doing experiments and taking photographs. They also had to repair their station. It was so badly damaged during its launch that, without repair, it would have been uninhabitable.

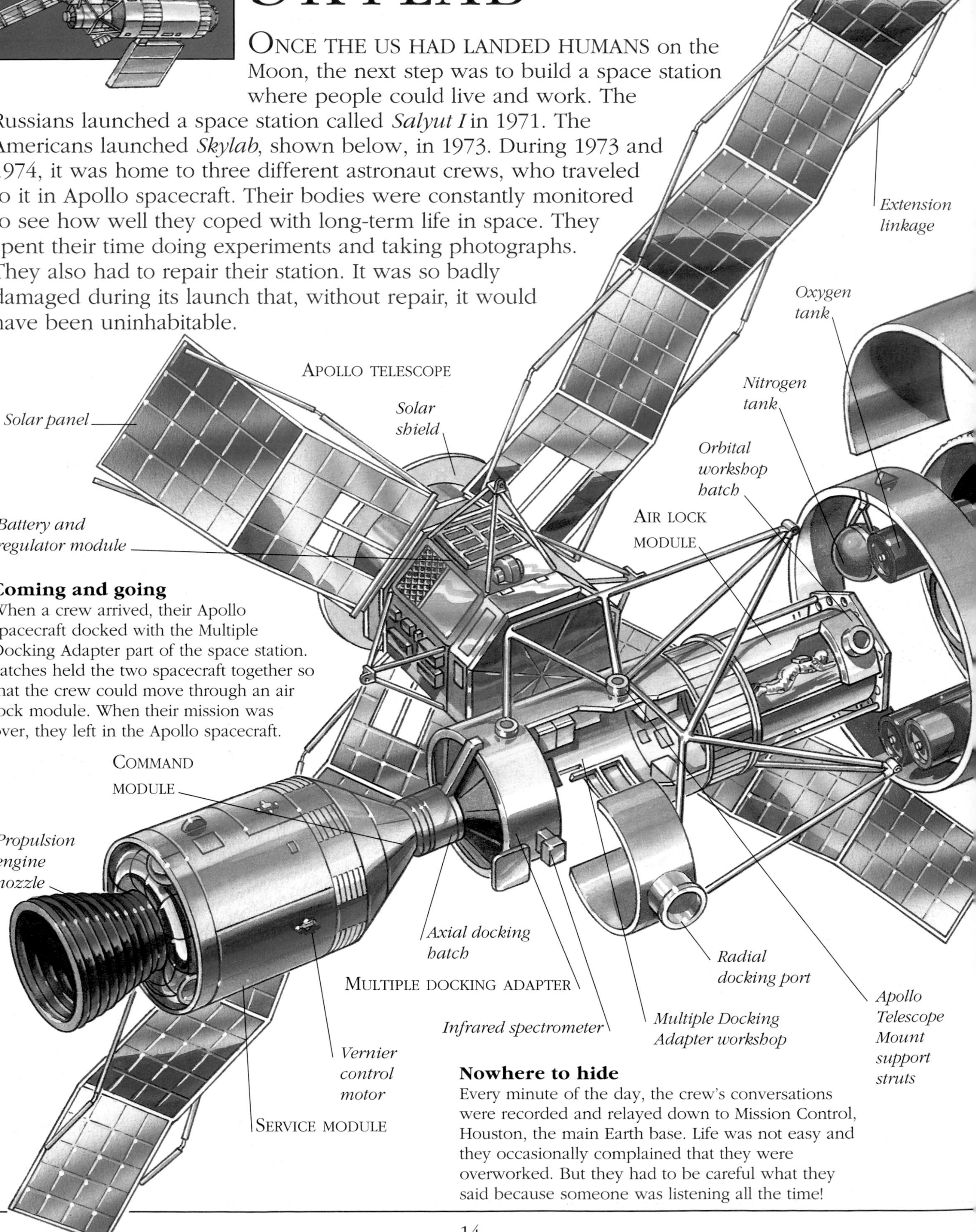

Coming and going

When a crew arrived, their Apollo spacecraft docked with the Multiple Docking Adapter part of the space station. Latches held the two spacecraft together so that the crew could move through an air lock module. When their mission was over, they left in the Apollo spacecraft.

Extension linkage

Oxygen tank

Nitrogen tank

APOLLO TELESCOPE

Solar shield

Orbital workshop hatch

Solar panel

AIR LOCK MODULE

Battery and regulator module

COMMAND MODULE

Propulsion engine nozzle

Axial docking hatch

MULTIPLE DOCKING ADAPTER

Radial docking port

Apollo Telescope Mount support struts

Infrared spectrometer

Multiple Docking Adapter workshop

Vernier control motor

SERVICE MODULE

Nowhere to hide

Every minute of the day, the crew's conversations were recorded and relayed down to Mission Control, Houston, the main Earth base. Life was not easy and they occasionally complained that they were overworked. But they had to be careful what they said because someone was listening all the time!

Energy savers

Skylab was fitted with huge solar arrays that converted the Sun's rays into electricity. During the launch one was torn off. Another jammed, leaving *Skylab* underpowered and overheated. Fortunately the first crew was able to unjam it and restore sufficient power to *Skylab*.

Solar array deployment boom

Solar array

Waste tank separation screen

Living in a space home

Skylab was built using the third stage of a *Saturn V* rocket. One of its fuel tanks was converted into a workshop with a wardroom for relaxing in, a sleeping compartment, a bathroom, and an experiment room. Food and clothing were stored on board, including 210 pairs of underpants.

Attitude control nitrogen bottle

Refrigeration system radiator

Control console

Shower cabinet

Sleep compartment

Micrometeoroid shield

ORBITAL WORKSHOP

Keeping fit

On board there was a treadmill and an exercise bicycle for the crew to keep fit. This is very important in space because when the body is weightless, muscles start to waste away. The *Skylab* astronauts had wobbly legs when they returned to Earth, but their muscles soon returned to normal.

Work, work, work

Above the station there was a platform called the Apollo Telescope Mount, which studied the Sun. The astronauts monitored its work and took photographs of the Earth. They made and tested metal, glass, and crystals to see if any developed differently in space.

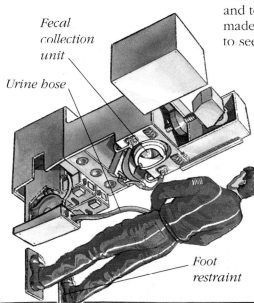

Fecal collection unit

Urine hose

PERSONAL HYGIENE STATION (SPACE TOILET)

Foot restraint

Space washing

In the bathroom there was a toilet that worked by vacuum suction. The waste was sucked away and stored so that the crew could take it back to Earth for study. An astronaut wanting a shower climbed into a collapsible tube device with a lid on the top to stop water globules from floating away.

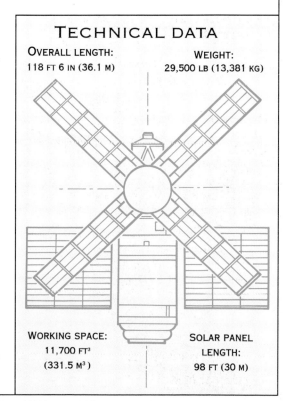

TECHNICAL DATA

OVERALL LENGTH:
118 FT 6 IN (36.1 M)

WEIGHT:
29,500 LB (13,381 KG)

WORKING SPACE:
11,700 FT³
(331.5 M³)

SOLAR PANEL LENGTH:
98 FT (30 M)

VIKING PROBE

UNMANNED SPACE PROBES are complex robot
explorers that journey far away to other
planets. They send back fascinating new
information and pictures. This is one
of two Viking probes, both
launched in 1975 toward the planet Mars.
People have always wondered about
outer space. Are there really Martians
living on Mars? The Viking probes
investigated puzzles like this by
surveying the planets and
searching for life-forms.

Landers at work

The landers carried computer-
controlled instruments
that analyzed the
landscape, wind, and
temperature. Each
lander had a remote-
controlled arm with a
shovel on the end for
collecting soil.

Landing the lander

Once separated from its orbiter, each
lander traveled down toward Mars. Near
the surface, its protective shell was ejected
and a parachute opened to slow the craft
down. Its legs unfolded and its rockets
ignited to give it a slow, soft landing.

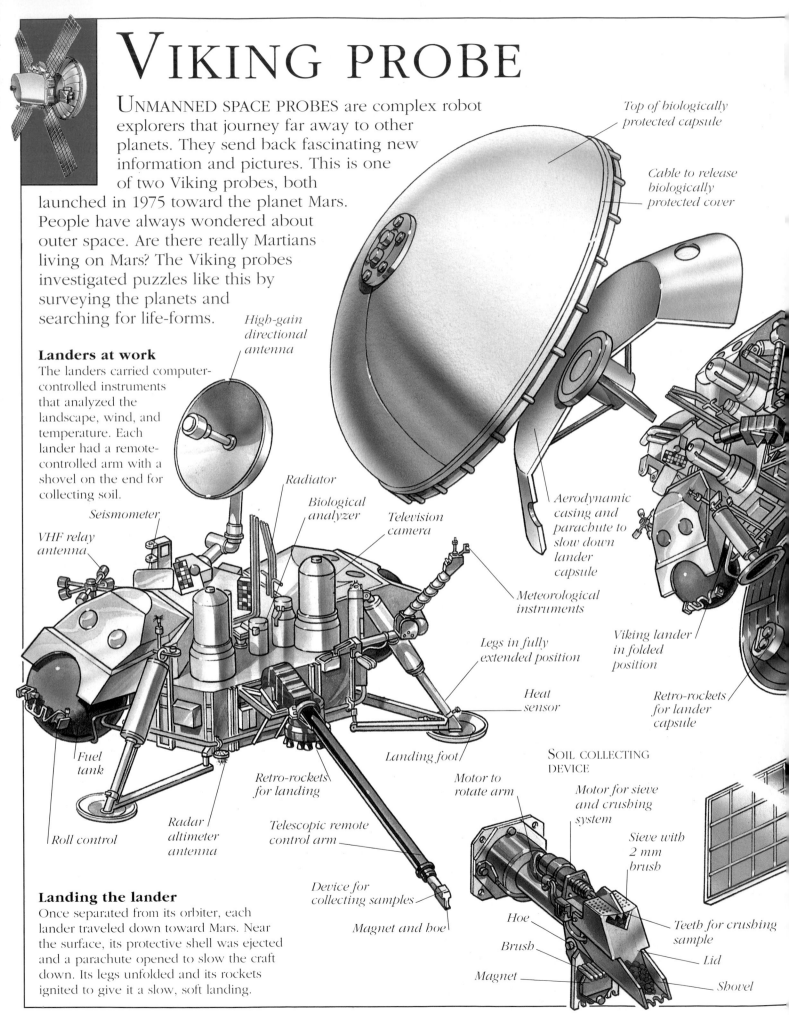

Top of biologically
protected capsule

Cable to release
biologically
protected cover

High-gain
directional
antenna

Aerodynamic
casing and
parachute to
slow down
lander
capsule

Radiator

Biological
analyzer

Television
camera

Meteorological
instruments

Seismometer

VHF relay
antenna

Legs in fully
extended position

Viking lander
in folded
position

Heat
sensor

Retro-rockets
for lander
capsule

Fuel
tank

Landing foot

Motor to
rotate arm

SOIL COLLECTING
DEVICE

Motor for sieve
and crushing
system

Roll control

Radar
altimeter
antenna

Retro-rockets
for landing

Telescopic remote
control arm

Sieve with
2 mm
brush

Device for
collecting samples

Hoe

Teeth for crushing
sample

Magnet and hoe

Brush

Lid

Magnet

Shovel

Viking parts

Each Viking probe was made up of two parts – the orbiter and the lander. The lander separated from the orbiter above Mars and landed on the surface. Meanwhile, the orbiter continued to circle the planet, recording pictures of the surface and relaying the information collected by the lander.

Attitude control micronozzles (gas jet)

Rock or roll?

Before the Viking missions scientists weren't sure whether the surface of Mars had a hard crust or a thick layer of soft dust that a Lander would sink down into. They found that it was hard and covered with chunks of rusty-red rock.

Infrared thermal mapper

Visual Imaging System

Solar panel

Fuel tank

Heat shield

Mars atmospheric water detector

TECHNICAL DATA

SOLAR PANELS TOTAL SURFACE AREA: 161 SQ/FT (15 SQ/M)

CENTRAL BODY DIAMETER: 12 FT (3.7 M)

EXTENDABLE ARM: 7 FT 6 IN (2.3 M)

TEN ELECTRONICS COMPARTMENTS EACH: 5 FT 10 IN (1.78 M) ACROSS, 18 IN (47 CM) HIGH

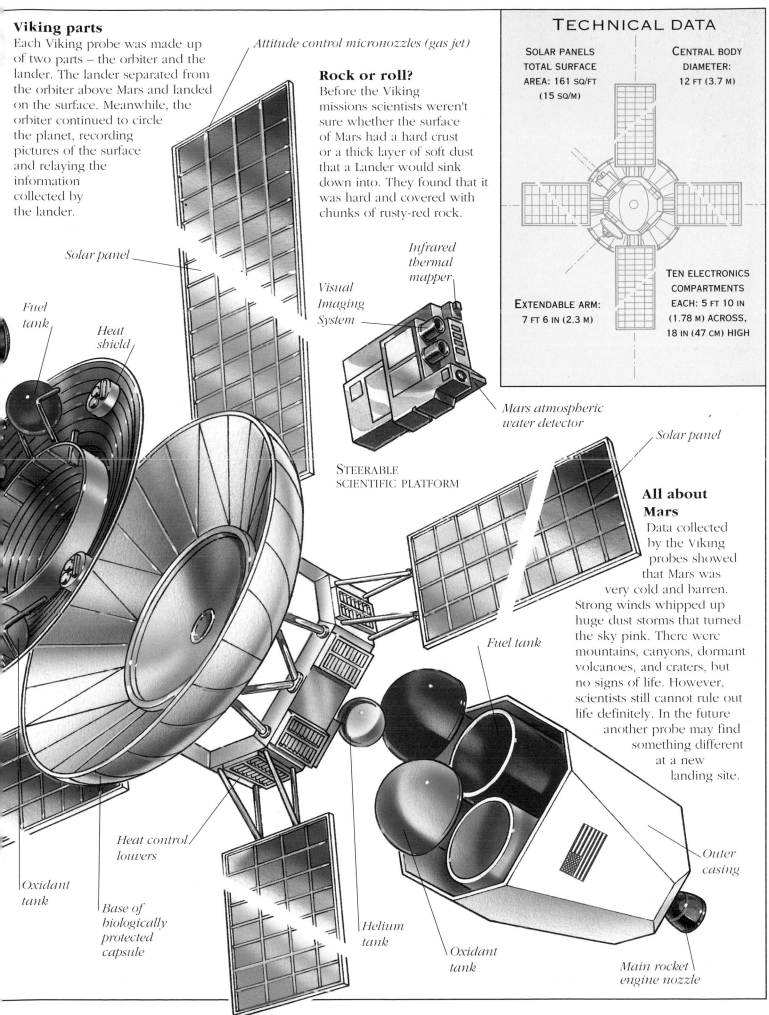

STEERABLE SCIENTIFIC PLATFORM

Solar panel

All about Mars

Data collected by the Viking probes showed that Mars was very cold and barren. Strong winds whipped up huge dust storms that turned the sky pink. There were mountains, canyons, dormant volcanoes, and craters, but no signs of life. However, scientists still cannot rule out life definitely. In the future another probe may find something different at a new landing site.

Fuel tank

Heat control louvers

Oxidant tank

Base of biologically protected capsule

Helium tank

Oxidant tank

Outer casing

Main rocket engine nozzle

SPACE SHUTTLE

THE FIRST US SPACE SHUTTLE was launched on April 12, 1981. The Shuttle is reusable, and since that first journey, many more missions have been flown, teaching astronauts a lot more about living and working in space. The Shuttle Orbiter is a cross between a space station and a space plane. People can live inside it as it orbits the Earth. It can land its crew safely back home and then, after being checked and refitted, it can fly on another mission. It is mainly used to launch satellites and to recover them for repair.

Getting up there

The plane part of the Shuttle, shown here, is called the Orbiter. When it is launched, it is attached to a fuel tank and two rocket boosters, which help lift it into orbit. After the launch, the boosters are jettisoned. They parachute back to Earth to be used again for another launch.

Getting to work

All the Orbiter's systems are controlled by computers. The crew checks these systems by looking at consoles on the flight deck, high up in the nose. The computers are constantly monitored by Mission Control back on Earth.

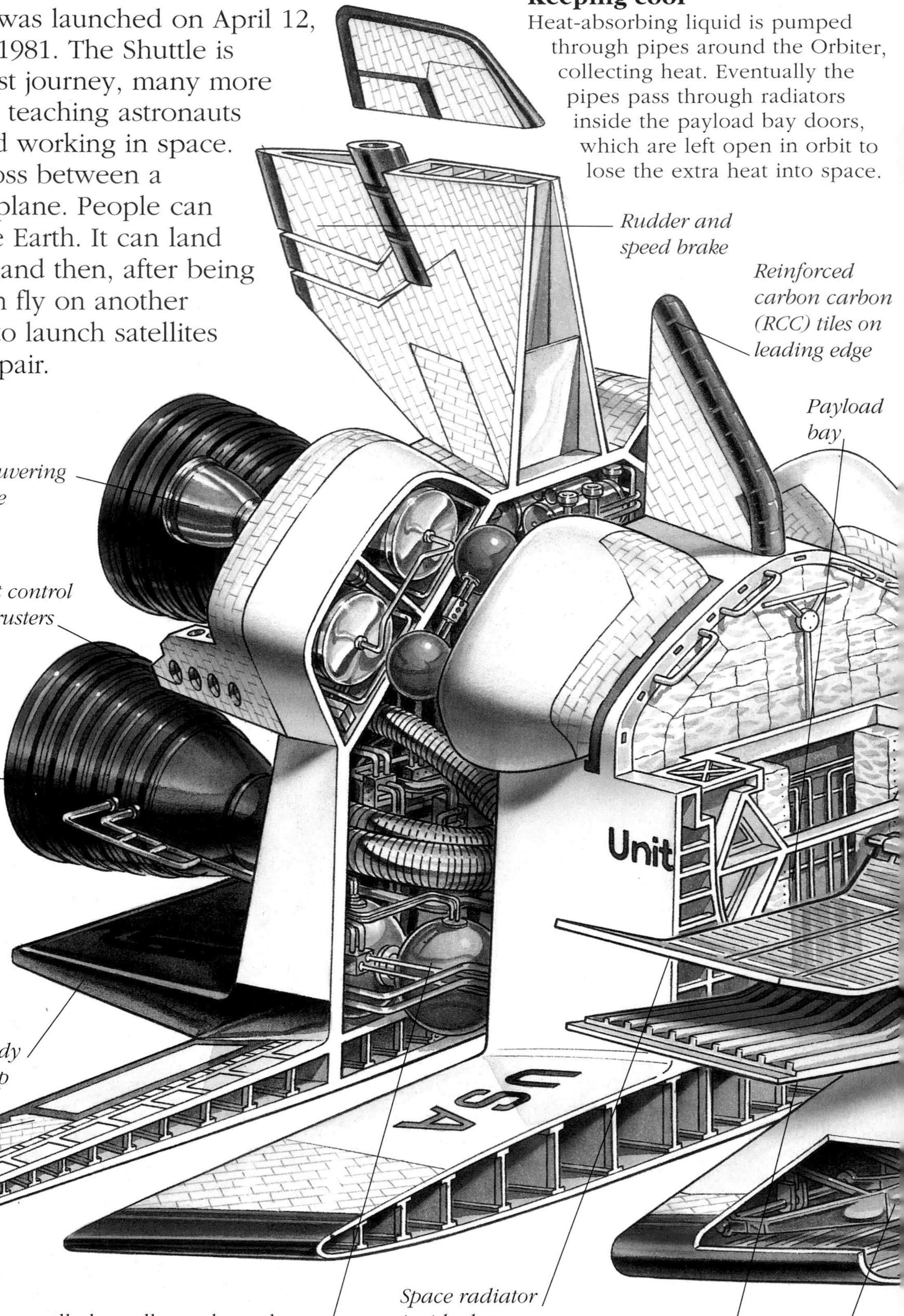

Keeping cool

Heat-absorbing liquid is pumped through pipes around the Orbiter, collecting heat. Eventually the pipes pass through radiators inside the payload bay doors, which are left open in orbit to lose the extra heat into space.

Rudder and speed brake

Reinforced carbon carbon (RCC) tiles on leading edge

Payload bay

Maneuvering engine

Aft control thrusters

Main engine

Body flap

Elevon

Unit

USA

Space radiator inside door

Payload bay door

Hydrazine and nitrogen tetroxide tank

Landing-gear well

Living on board

Astronauts have a miniature kitchen called a galley, where they heat up their food in pre-packed containers. Four people can rest in the "sleep station," strapping themselves into sleeping bags. One sleeps upside down and one sleeps standing up. Because they are weightless, it feels no different than normal.

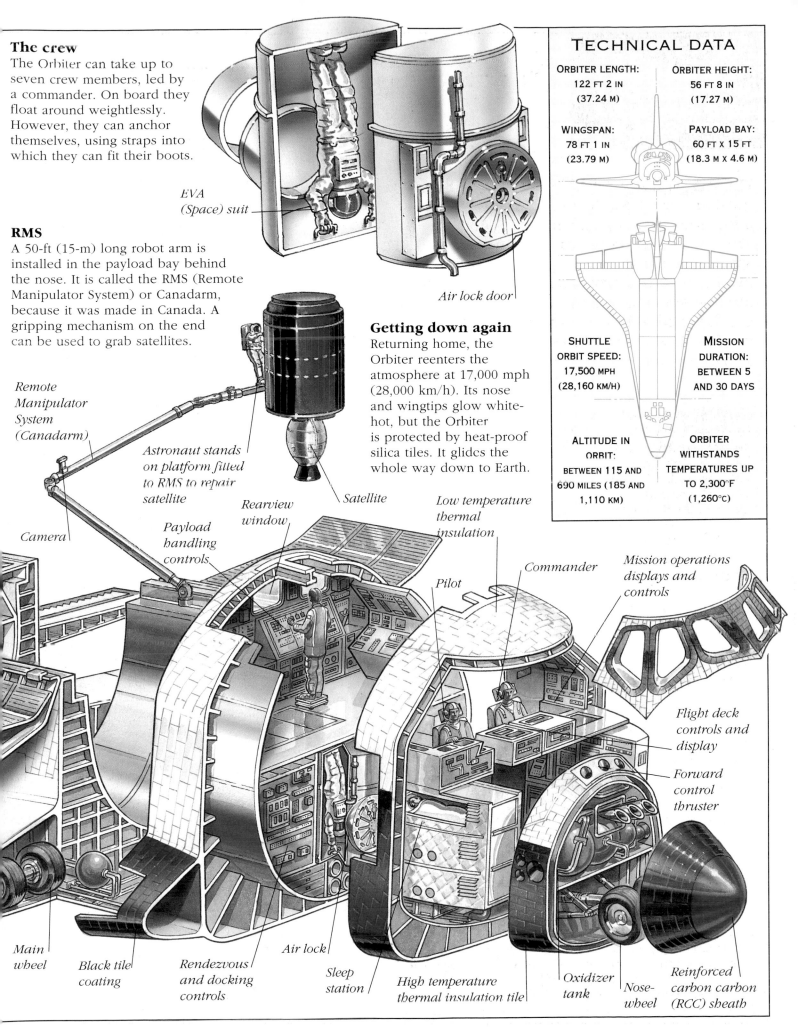

The crew

The Orbiter can take up to seven crew members, led by a commander. On board they float around weightlessly. However, they can anchor themselves, using straps into which they can fit their boots.

RMS

A 50-ft (15-m) long robot arm is installed in the payload bay behind the nose. It is called the RMS (Remote Manipulator System) or Canadarm, because it was made in Canada. A gripping mechanism on the end can be used to grab satellites.

Remote Manipulator System (Canadarm)

EVA (Space) suit

Air lock door

Astronaut stands on platform fitted to RMS to repair satellite

Satellite

Getting down again

Returning home, the Orbiter reenters the atmosphere at 17,000 mph (28,000 km/h). Its nose and wingtips glow white-hot, but the Orbiter is protected by heat-proof silica tiles. It glides the whole way down to Earth.

Camera

Payload handling controls

Rearview window

Low temperature thermal insulation

Pilot

Commander

Mission operations displays and controls

Flight deck controls and display

Forward control thruster

Main wheel

Black tile coating

Rendezvous and docking controls

Air lock

Sleep station

High temperature thermal insulation tile

Oxidizer tank

Nose-wheel

Reinforced carbon carbon (RCC) sheath

TECHNICAL DATA

ORBITER LENGTH: 122 FT 2 IN (37.24 M)

ORBITER HEIGHT: 56 FT 8 IN (17.27 M)

WINGSPAN: 78 FT 1 IN (23.79 M)

PAYLOAD BAY: 60 FT X 15 FT (18.3 M X 4.6 M)

SHUTTLE ORBIT SPEED: 17,500 MPH (28,160 KM/H)

MISSION DURATION: BETWEEN 5 AND 30 DAYS

ALTITUDE IN ORBIT: BETWEEN 115 AND 690 MILES (185 AND 1,110 KM)

ORBITER WITHSTANDS TEMPERATURES UP TO 2,300°F (1,260°C)

SPACE WALK

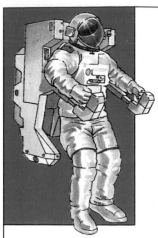

SOMETIMES ASTRONAUTS HAVE TO VENTURE outside of a Shuttle to capture and repair satellites or to test new equipment. But they would die a quick, painful death if they were not properly equipped. Going outside is called "extra-vehicular activity," or EVA. An astronaut on EVA must wear a complicated space suit for protection, to maintain pressure, and to provide air for breathing. Until recently, astronauts on EVA had to be tethered to their spacecraft with a cable. Otherwise they would float away, and it would be very hard to rescue them. Now they can use a "Manned Maneuvering Unit," or MMU. Shaped like the top part of an armchair, with arms and a back support, it jets the astronauts wherever they want to go.

Automatic TV camera

Nitrogen gas tank

Nitrogen gas tank holder

Strong metal ring locks suit parts together

TECHNICAL DATA

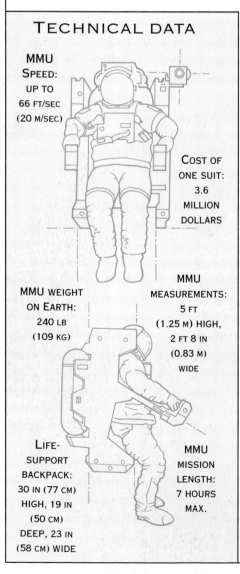

MMU
SPEED:
UP TO
66 FT/SEC
(20 M/SEC)

COST OF
ONE SUIT:
3.6
MILLION
DOLLARS

MMU WEIGHT
ON EARTH:
240 LB
(109 KG)

MMU
MEASUREMENTS:
5 FT
(1.25 M) HIGH,
2 FT 8 IN
(0.83 M)
WIDE

LIFE-
SUPPORT
BACKPACK:
30 IN (77 CM)
HIGH, 19 IN
(50 CM)
DEEP, 23 IN
(58 CM) WIDE

MMU
MISSION
LENGTH:
7 HOURS
MAX.

Astronaut underwear
Because astronauts can spend many hours inside their space suits, the first thing they put on is a urine collection device. Next they pull on a cooling suit with a network of water-filled tubes. The water absorbs body heat, which the tubes circulate to the space suit's backpack, where it radiates out into space.

Directional nitrogen gas nozzle

Liquid cooling and vent undergarment

Tube carrying cooling water

Outer suit pants

Overshoe

Astronaut outerwear
The outer suit has parts that lock together with airtight metal rings. Made from many layers of nylon material, it has pleats in it that stretch to fit an astronaut's body. The inside of the suit is pumped full of air to keep the astronaut's body pressurized.

Holes in socks keep astronaut's feet cool

Life-support backpack with oxygen supply and water for cooling system

Helmet

Headphones

Sunglasses

Microphone

Back and front

Suits are called "extra-vehicular mobility units," or EMU's. A life-support pack on the back carries enough oxygen for a seven-hour trip. A computer in the chest pack monitors the way the suit is working.

Heart rate and breathing monitor

Visor shields face from the Sun

Clear plastic helmet rubbed with anti-fogging compound to keep it from misting up

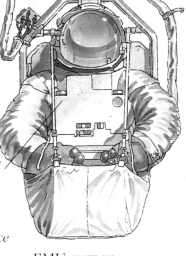

EMU SUIT IN STORAGE POSITION

A bad idea

If you went on a space walk without a pressurized space suit, your blood and body fluids would quickly begin to boil. You would inflate like a balloon, suffocate, and nitrogen bubbles would cut off the blood supply to your brain.

Moving the MMU

The MMU has 24 small nozzles called thrusters. The hand controls on the arms are used to make nitrogen gas jet out of the thrusters, pushing the MMU.

Chest pack with computer controls and LED display

Gloves

Adjustable arm

Outside made of space suit material

RESCUE BALL

Face mask

Left-hand joystick unit for making the MMU go backward or forward

Oxygen from life-support system enters suit here

Oxygen respirator

Carrying handle

Space rescue!

Shuttle orbiters have only three full EMU suits on board, but carry a crew of 7. In case something goes wrong and a Shuttle crew has to abandon ship, the space rescue ball has been designed to help the rest of the crew escape. It is made from space suit material, and holds an oxygen supply so that an astronaut can be safely evacuated to another waiting Shuttle.

ARIANE 4

IN FRENCH GUIANA, SOUTH AMERICA, a massive launch site has been cut out of the surrounding jungle. This is the base for the European Ariane rockets, the workhorses of space. They regularly launch satellites into orbit around the Earth. They are "commercial space carriers," which means that any country can hire them to have satellites carried up and released. This picture shows the rocket most often used – the *Ariane 4*. It has three stages that separate from each other during flight, on the same principle as the *Saturn V* rocket on page 8/9. But unlike the *Saturn V,* it is an "off-the-peg" rocket – it comes in six different sizes.

Command by computer
Ariane rockets rely completely on onboard computers. They command the rocket stages to separate by triggering small explosive charges around the top of each stage, and they command all the different engines to fire at the right times.

Booster rockets
The biggest versions of *Ariane 4* have extra booster rockets attached to stage 1, so they have extra pushing power to launch heavy satellites. Some have two boosters; some have four.

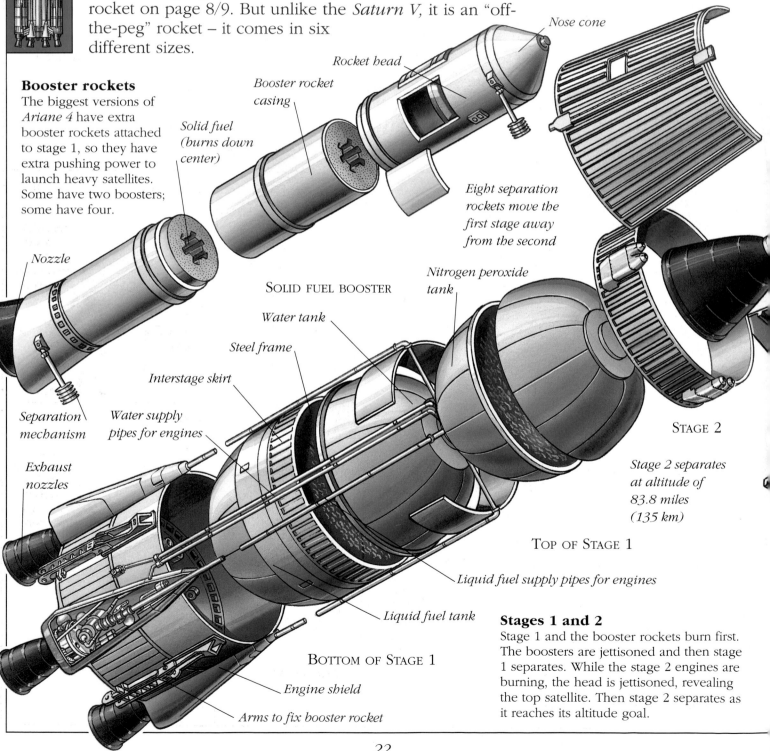

Rocket head

Booster rocket casing

Nose cone

Solid fuel (burns down center)

Eight separation rockets move the first stage away from the second

Nozzle

SOLID FUEL BOOSTER

Nitrogen peroxide tank

Water tank

Steel frame

Interstage skirt

Separation mechanism

Water supply pipes for engines

Exhaust nozzles

STAGE 2

Stage 2 separates at altitude of 83.8 miles (135 km)

TOP OF STAGE 1

Liquid fuel supply pipes for engines

Liquid fuel tank

BOTTOM OF STAGE 1

Engine shield

Arms to fix booster rocket

Stages 1 and 2
Stage 1 and the booster rockets burn first. The boosters are jettisoned and then stage 1 separates. While the stage 2 engines are burning, the head is jettisoned, revealing the top satellite. Then stage 2 separates as it reaches its altitude goal.

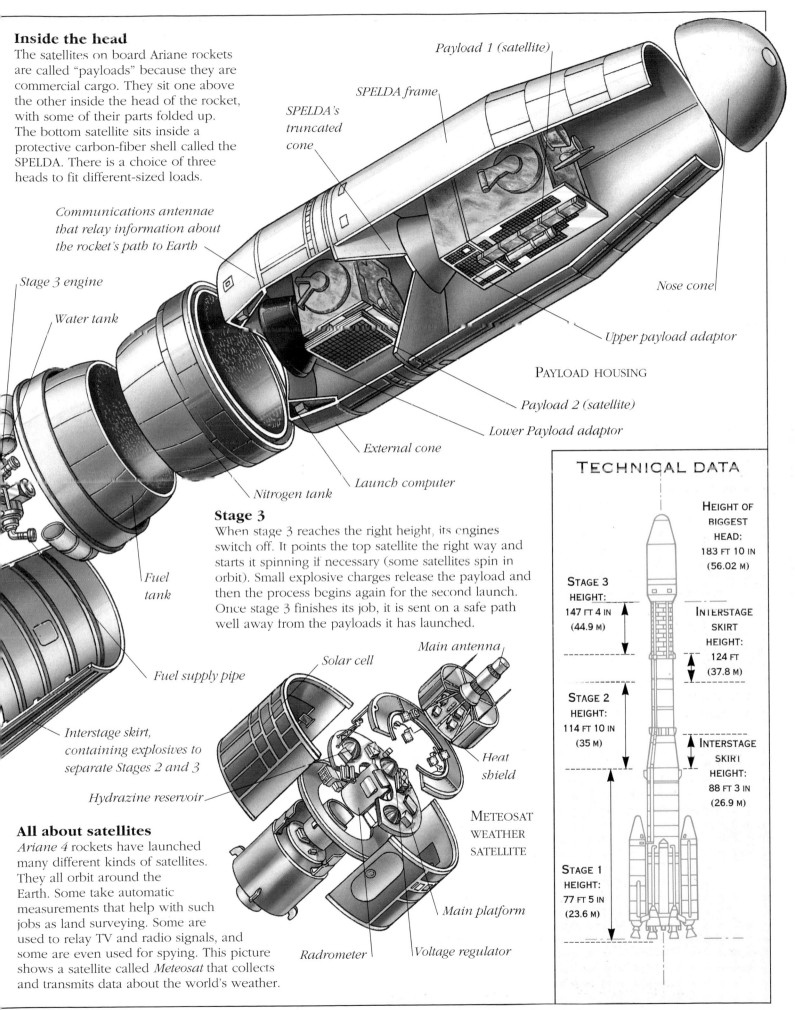

Inside the head

The satellites on board Ariane rockets are called "payloads" because they are commercial cargo. They sit one above the other inside the head of the rocket, with some of their parts folded up. The bottom satellite sits inside a protective carbon-fiber shell called the SPELDA. There is a choice of three heads to fit different-sized loads.

Communications antennae that relay information about the rocket's path to Earth

Stage 3 engine

Water tank

Fuel tank

Fuel supply pipe

Interstage skirt, containing explosives to separate Stages 2 and 3

Hydrazine reservoir

Payload 1 (satellite)

SPELDA frame

SPELDA's truncated cone

Nose cone

Upper payload adaptor

PAYLOAD HOUSING

Payload 2 (satellite)

Lower Payload adaptor

External cone

Launch computer

Nitrogen tank

Stage 3

When stage 3 reaches the right height, its engines switch off. It points the top satellite the right way and starts it spinning if necessary (some satellites spin in orbit). Small explosive charges release the payload and then the process begins again for the second launch. Once stage 3 finishes its job, it is sent on a safe path well away from the payloads it has launched.

Solar cell

Main antenna

Heat shield

METEOSAT WEATHER SATELLITE

Main platform

Radrometer

Voltage regulator

All about satellites

Ariane 4 rockets have launched many different kinds of satellites. They all orbit around the Earth. Some take automatic measurements that help with such jobs as land surveying. Some are used to relay TV and radio signals, and some are even used for spying. This picture shows a satellite called Meteosat *that collects and transmits data about the world's weather.*

TECHNICAL DATA

HEIGHT OF BIGGEST HEAD: 183 FT 10 IN (56.02 M)

STAGE 3 HEIGHT: 147 FT 4 IN (44.9 M)

INTERSTAGE SKIRT HEIGHT: 124 FT (37.8 M)

STAGE 2 HEIGHT: 114 FT 10 IN (35 M)

INTERSTAGE SKIRT HEIGHT: 88 FT 3 IN (26.9 M)

STAGE 1 HEIGHT: 77 FT 5 IN (23.6 M)

VOYAGER

TWO VOYAGERS, 1 AND 2, were launched in 1977, beginning an exciting long-distance journey into deep space. They were sent to the outer reaches of the Solar System where they found strange frozen moons and giant planets enveloped in poisonous gases. They are still traveling onward through outer space, carrying a message from Earth to any intelligent beings.

Radioisotope thermoelectric generators

On board the Voyagers
The Voyagers are controlled by computers. Their scientific instruments measure such things as magnetic fields, and their cameras send back spectacular images of the planets.

Magnetometer

Extendable arm

Dish antenna

Magnetometers

Fuel tank

Electronics packs

The journey so far
Both Voyagers were launched in 1977. They flew past Jupiter in 1979 and went on to Saturn, which they reached in 1980/81. By this time they were so far away their radio signals took 1.5 hours to reach Earth. *Voyager 2* flew past Uranus in 1986 and Neptune in 1989.

Reflecting dish base

Aluminum framework

Antenna inside dish

Reflecting dish

TV cameras to photograph moons and planets

Cosmic ray detector

Plasma detector

Amazing space
The Voyager probes have made many amazing discoveries on their journey past the outer planets. The spectacular pictures they have sent show new moons and planet rings. The "Great Red Spot" that astronomers had noticed on Jupiter turned out to be a gigantic swirling storm of deadly gas clouds.

Steerable platform

Scientific instruments to collect various data, including gases, rays, and particles around planets

TECHNICAL DATA

DISH ANTENNA DIAMETER:
12 FT (3.7 M)

10-SIDED FRAME

EXTENDABLE ARM:
7 FT 6 IN (2.3 M)

10 ELECTRONICS COMPARTMENTS:
5 FT 10 IN (1.78 M) ACROSS,
18 IN (47 CM) HIGH

GIOTTO PROBE

GIOTTO WAS LAUNCHED IN 1985 AND, IN 1986, it passed close to Halley's Comet, taking measurements and pictures as it went. Halley's Comet is an object that orbits the Sun, passing the Earth every 76 years. For many centuries people thought it was a magical sign that heralded some great change. Scientists in modern times just wanted to find out what it was made of.

Main body made to spin 15 times a minute to stabilize Giotto *in space*

Giotto's job

Giotto was sent to examine the comet's nucleus (its center). The probe passed within 375 miles (605 km) of the nucleus, transmitting information back to Earth as it traveled by. When it got in close, it was hit by a giant jet of dust that knocked it off course and damaged its instruments. But by that time it had already sent back lots of valuable data.

Shell to close off engine nozzle after use (to stop comet particles from getting in)

Camera

Tripod

Magnetometer experiment for measuring the comet's magnetic field

Antenna for receiving command signals from Earth

Dish antenna for sending data to Earth

Mechanism to stop the dish antenna from spinning with the main body

Solar cells

Hydrazine tank

Fuel tank for rocket engine

Attitude control thrusters

Rocket engine to get Giotto *into orbit after its launch*

Lower platform

Shield to protect from buffeting

Giotto's experiments

On its lower platform *Giotto* carried instruments for monitoring the comet. These included a camera and impact detectors to measure the buffeting that *Giotto* got from the dust and ice particles around the comet. All the information was transmitted back to Earth.

Comet profile

Giotto found that Halley's Comet is really a kind of giant dirty snowball. Its solid peanut-shaped spinning nucleus is made of water and dust. Jets of dust, gas, and ice particles spew out of cracks in its crust as it gets heated up by the Sun. These jets reflect the Sun's light, so they look like a glowing tail streaming out behind it.

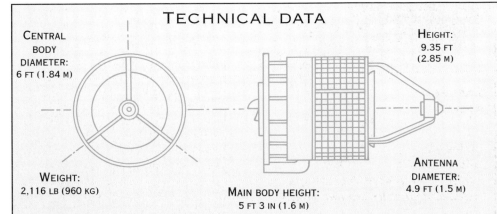

TECHNICAL DATA

CENTRAL BODY DIAMETER: 6 FT (1.84 M)

HEIGHT: 9.35 FT (2.85 M)

WEIGHT: 2,116 LB (960 KG)

MAIN BODY HEIGHT: 5 FT 3 IN (1.6 M)

ANTENNA DIAMETER: 4.9 FT (1.5 M)

HUBBLE TELESCOPE

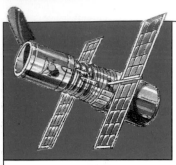

IN 1990 A NASA SPACE SHUTTLE launched a satellite called *Hubble*. It was a space telescope designed to peer into the far reaches of space and relay back information. Telescopes on Earth must look through the cloudy, dusty atmosphere, which blurs their vision. *Hubble* orbits above the atmosphere and so can see much farther. When *Hubble* was first launched, the images it sent back were very fuzzy. As well, its solar arrays (panels on either side) often shook badly. So NASA sent another Shuttle to make the most expensive repairs yet in space history.

Aperture door mounting

Communications antenna

Primary mirror

Light shield

Radial SI module (1)

Secondary baffle

Central deflector

Secondary mirror

Optical telescope assembly

Aluminum shield

Epoxy resin frame

What does it do?
Hubble detects and measures the light given out by galaxies and stars. Some forms of light can be seen. Others, such as infrared rays and ultraviolet rays, can't be seen but can still be measured. When *Hubble's* mirror is pointed at an object sending out light, the light is focused onto various instruments inside the satellite, where it is measured.

Getting information
Hubble converts the data it collects into radio signals. It sends these to a communications satellite, which sends them on to Earth. Computers on Earth convert them into electronically made images that astronomers can study.

Aperture door

Aperture

SUPPORT SYSTEM MODULE

Crew handrails

Picking up the past
Some of the objects that *Hubble* sees are so far away that their light takes millions of years to arrive. The pictures that *Hubble* produces from this ancient light show a time when the universe was much younger than it is today. Scientists may be able to use them to figure out when the universe began and how big it is.

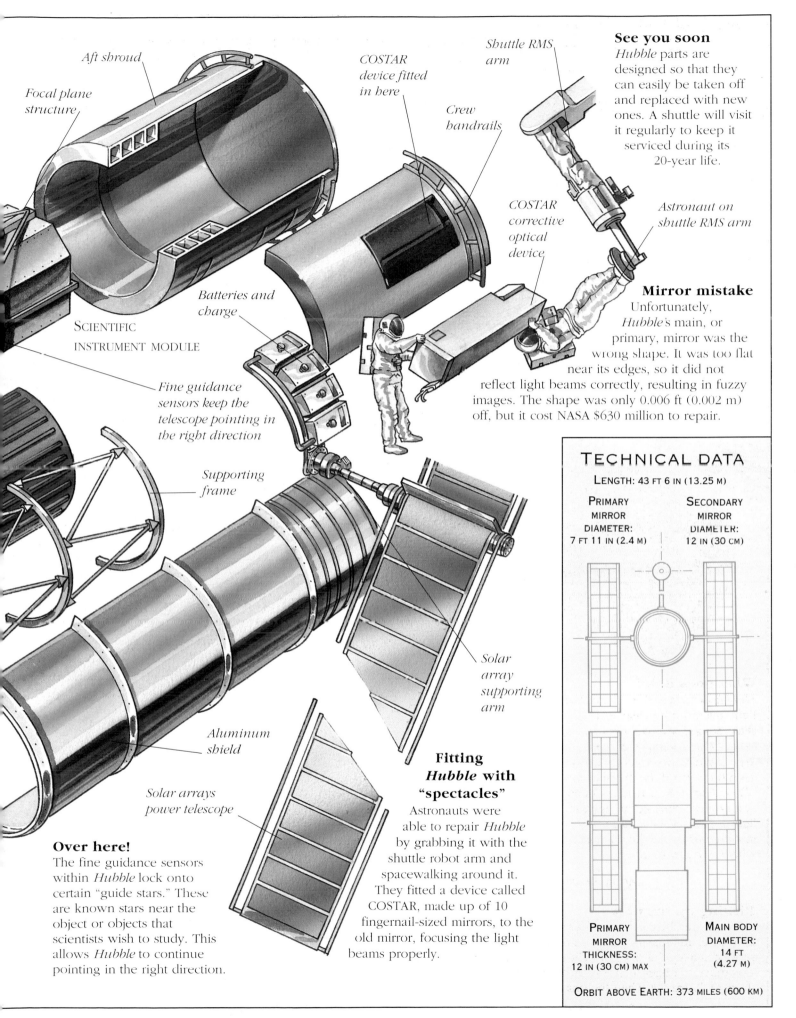

Aft shroud

Focal plane
structure

COSTAR
device fitted
in here

Crew
handrails

Shuttle RMS
arm

See you soon
Hubble parts are
designed so that they
can easily be taken off
and replaced with new
ones. A shuttle will visit
it regularly to keep it
serviced during its
20-year life.

COSTAR
corrective
optical
device

Astronaut on
shuttle RMS arm

SCIENTIFIC
INSTRUMENT MODULE

Batteries and
charge

Mirror mistake
Unfortunately,
Hubble's main, or
primary, mirror was the
wrong shape. It was too flat
near its edges, so it did not
reflect light beams correctly, resulting in fuzzy
images. The shape was only 0.006 ft (0.002 m)
off, but it cost NASA $630 million to repair.

Fine guidance
sensors keep the
telescope pointing in
the right direction

Supporting
frame

TECHNICAL DATA

LENGTH: 43 FT 6 IN (13.25 M)

PRIMARY MIRROR DIAMETER: 7 FT 11 IN (2.4 M)	SECONDARY MIRROR DIAMETER: 12 IN (30 CM)

Aluminum
shield

Solar
array
supporting
arm

Solar arrays
power telescope

**Fitting
Hubble with
"spectacles"**
Astronauts were
able to repair *Hubble*
by grabbing it with the
shuttle robot arm and
spacewalking around it.
They fitted a device called
COSTAR, made up of 10
fingernail-sized mirrors, to the
old mirror, focusing the light
beams properly.

Over here!
The fine guidance sensors
within *Hubble* lock onto
certain "guide stars." These
are known stars near the
object or objects that
scientists wish to study. This
allows *Hubble* to continue
pointing in the right direction.

PRIMARY MIRROR THICKNESS: 12 IN (30 CM) MAX	MAIN BODY DIAMETER: 14 FT (4.27 M)

ORBIT ABOVE EARTH: 373 MILES (600 KM)

SPACE TIMELINE

HUMANS DID NOT BEGIN to explore space until the twentieth century. In the beginning, small unmanned rockets and satellites were used. Since then, spacecraft have developed into the most complex and expensive machines ever built. Here are some milestones in the development of modern spacecraft.

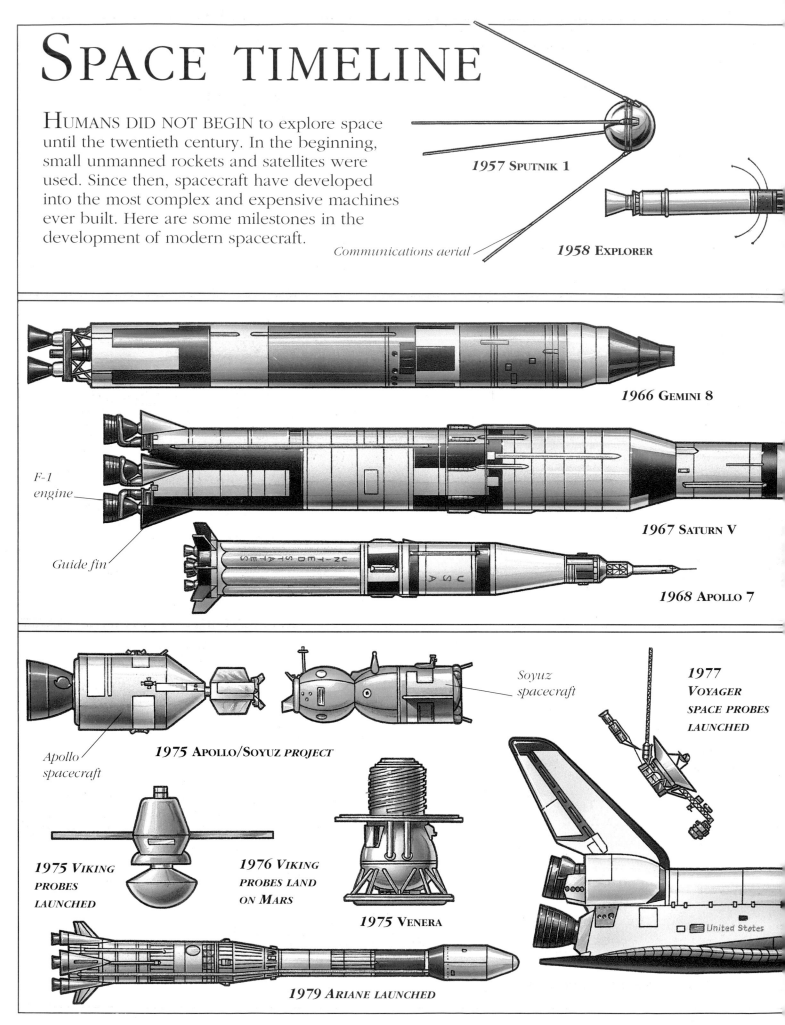

1957 SPUTNIK 1

1958 EXPLORER

Communications aerial

1966 GEMINI 8

F-1 engine

1967 SATURN V

Guide fin

1968 APOLLO 7

Apollo spacecraft

1975 APOLLO/SOYUZ *PROJECT*

Soyuz spacecraft

1977 VOYAGER SPACE PROBES LAUNCHED

1975 VIKING PROBES LAUNCHED

1976 VIKING PROBES LAND ON MARS

1975 VENERA

United States

1979 ARIANE LAUNCHED

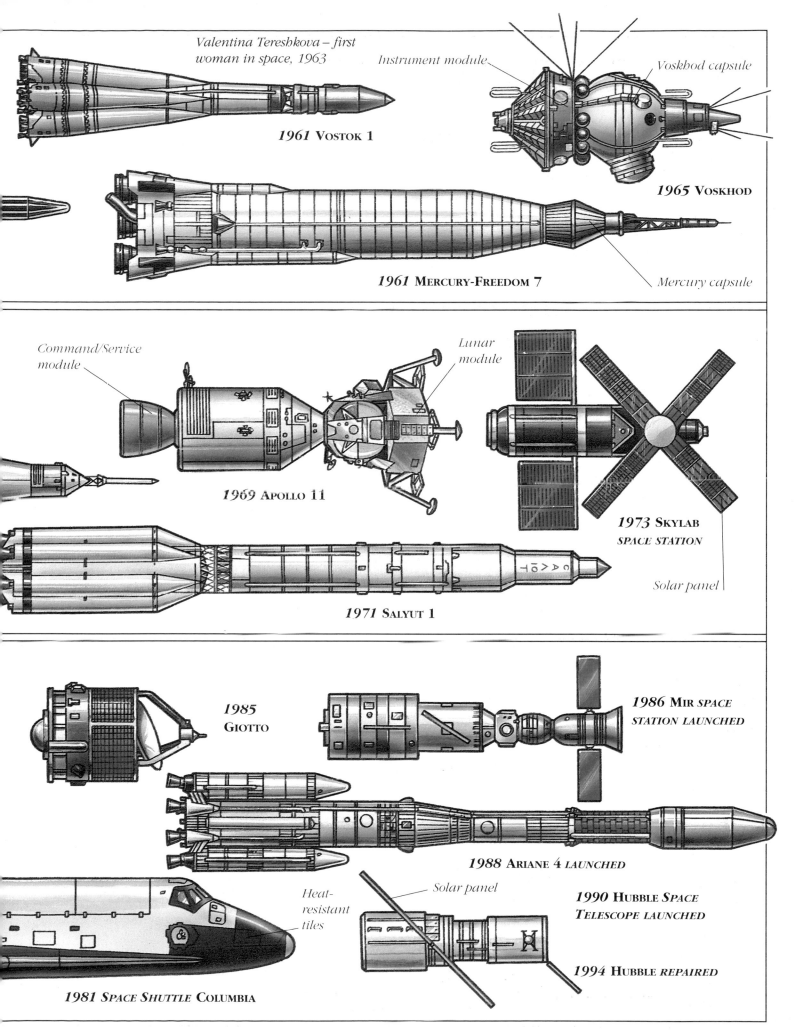

Valentina Tereshkova – first woman in space, 1963

1961 VOSTOK 1

Instrument module

Voskhod capsule

1965 VOSKHOD

1961 MERCURY-FREEDOM 7

Mercury capsule

Command/Service module

Lunar module

1969 APOLLO 11

1973 SKYLAB
SPACE STATION

Solar panel

1971 SALYUT 1

1985 GIOTTO

1986 MIR *SPACE STATION LAUNCHED*

1988 ARIANE 4 *LAUNCHED*

Heat-resistant tiles

Solar panel

1990 HUBBLE SPACE TELESCOPE LAUNCHED

1994 HUBBLE *REPAIRED*

1981 SPACE SHUTTLE COLUMBIA

GLOSSARY

Air lock
A space between an inner and outer door on a manned spacecraft. Crew members usually put on space suits here. Then they close the inner door tightly and let out all the air from the air lock. Only then can they open the outer door. If they didn't use an air lock, all the air in the craft would be sucked out into space when they went outside.

Air lock
External door
Internal door
Crew compartment

Antenna
A dish or rod aerial for receiving and sending radio signals to and from Earth.

Booster rockets
Extra rockets fitted onto a bigger launch rocket to help it gain extra speed as it travels up into space.

Command and Service Module
CSM for short. Part of an Apollo spacecraft. It orbited around the Moon with one crew member on board while the other crew members landed on the Moon's surface in the Lunar Module.

Console
A dashboard display with controls and switches for a space crew to use.

Delta wing
A swept-back wing shaped like a giant V, used on the space shuttle.

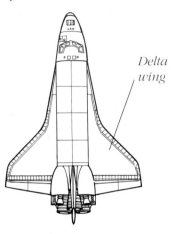

Delta wing

Depressurized
A place is depressurized when all the air is removed from it. For instance, air locks are depressurized when astronauts are ready to go outside on a space walk.

Docking
One spacecraft joining up with another in space.

Docking adaptor
The part of a spacecraft designed to lock onto another spacecraft when they dock together.

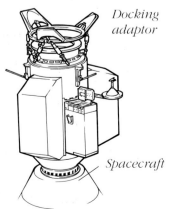

Docking adaptor
Spacecraft

Docking hatch
A hatch that can be opened between two docked spacecraft, so that crew members can move through from one to the other.

Extra-vehicular mobility unit
EMU for short. Space jargon for a space suit.

Extra-vehicular activity
EVA for short. Space jargon for a space walk.

Fuel
The substance needed to make rocket engines work. Some fuel is liquid, some is solid and rubbery. It is burned together with a substance called an "oxidizer" to make gases that rush out of engine nozzles, pushing a launch rocket or spacecraft forward.

Heat shield
A protective layer of heat-resistant material built around a spacecraft. This is particularly important if a manned spacecraft returns to Earth, because as it plunges down, the outside surfaces get very hot and the crew needs to be protected inside the cabin.

Life-support system
Equipment that provides crew members with the air, water, and warmth they need to survive in space.

Lunar Module
LM for short. The part of an Apollo spacecraft that landed on the Moon.

Lunar Roving Vehicle
LRV for short. A battery-powered buggy used for driving over the surface of the Moon.

Mission Control
The main space center on Earth where scientists monitor a spacecraft and keep in contact with the crew members on board.

Manned Maneuvering Unit
MMU for short. A rocket-powered backpack used by astronauts to fly around outside their spacecraft.

NASA
The National Aeronautics and Space Administration. The organization in charge of space exploration on behalf of the United States, founded in 1958 by President Eisenhower.

Nose cone
The top part of a launch rocket. Manned spacecraft or satellites sit inside the nose cone while they are being taken up into space.

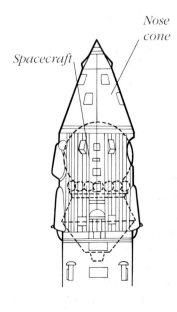

Nose cone
Spacecraft

Orbit

A circular path followed by a small object revolving around a larger object, such as a satellite revolving around the Earth or an Apollo spacecraft revolving around the Moon.

Orbit

Oxidizer

A substance (usually a gas) that is burned together with fuel to drive a rocket engine.

Payload

A commercial cargo, such as a satellite, carried on board a spacecraft. Customers pay to send it into space.

Personal hygiene station

The bathroom/toilet on board a spacecraft.

Pressure suit

A simple form of space suit sometimes worn inside the cabin of a spacecraft. It protects crew members in case the cabin loses its air supply during a critical part of the mission, such as launching or landing.

Pressurized

A place is pressurized when it is filled with air. Spacecraft cabins and space suits are pressurized to imitate the pressure existing in the atmosphere around the Earth.

Reaction-control system

Controls, usually mini rocket nozzles, which are used to change a spacecraft's position in space.

Reentry

The point when a spacecraft reenters the Earth's atmosphere on the way home. At this stage, air molecules start to rub against the craft as it falls, making its outer surface very hot.

Reentry

Remote Manipulator System

(RMS for short, also called Canadarm.) The robot arm attached to a space shuttle. It is used for jobs such as launching and repairing satellites. It was made in Canada.

Rocket

An engine that carries its own fuel and oxygen so that it can work in space as well as in the atmosphere. It is pushed upward by gases streaming out of its exhaust nozzles. Launch vehicles are made up of several rocket stages linked together.

Remote sensing instruments

Equipment that measures different kinds of radiation. These instruments are fitted to spacecraft to do various jobs.

Satellite

A satellite is something that circles (orbits) around a much larger object. Artificial space satellites are unmanned. They orbit the Earth doing different jobs, such as relaying telephone calls or surveying and measuring the landscape.

Satellite

Sleep station

The crew sleeping quarters on board a manned spacecraft.

Solar array

A wing shape covered in a sheet of solar cells. These collect sunlight and convert it into electricity, which can be used to run equipment on a spacecraft.

Space probe

An unmanned spacecraft sent to gather information about other planets and stars. Some space probes land, such as *Viking*. Some, such as *Voyager*, fly past planets, collecting information as they go.

Space station

A manned spacecraft that orbits the Earth. Crew members can live and work on board for long periods of time.

Space lab

A laboratory workshop situated in the shuttle cargo bay. Scientific experiments are carried out in this lab by astronauts up in space.

Splashdown

The moment when a manned spacecraft hits the water, if it splashes down in the ocean on its return to Earth.

MERCURY SPLASHDOWN

Parachute

Air-filled skirt cushions impact

Recovery helicopter

Splashdown

INDEX

A B

airbags, 12
air lock, 7, 14
antennae, 7
Apollo 8, 9, 11
Apollo 11, 8-13
Apollo 13, 13
Apollo 17, 11
Ariane 4, 22-23
Armstrong, Neil, 10
ascent stage, 10
astronauts, 6, 9, 10, 11, 18, 20
    see also crew

booster rockets, 18, 22

C

cabin, *Apollo 11*, 10, 13
Canadarm, 19
CM, 9, 10, 14
Command and Service Modules (CSM), 12, 13
Command Module (CM), 9, 10, 14
commercial space carrier, 22
communications antennae, 7
cosmonauts, 7
COSTAR, 27
crew,
    Apollo 11, 10-13
    Skylab, 14, 15
    Space Shuttle, 18, 19
    see also astronauts
CSM, 12, 13

D

descent stage, 10
Docking Adapter, 14

E

"Eagle," 10
EMU, 21
engines, 8, 13

escape tower, 9
EVA, 20
extra-vehicular activity (EVA), 20
extra-vehicular mobility unit (EMU), 21

F

Fitness, space, 15
Friendship 7, 6

G

Gagarin, Yuri, 7
galley, 18
Giotto probe, 25
Glenn, John, 6

H

Halley's Comet, 25
heat shield, 6
heat-proof tiles, 19
Hubble telescope, 26-27
hygiene station, 15

J

Jupiter, 24

L

lander, 16, 17
launcher, 8
Leonov, Alexei, 7
life-support backpack, 21
liftoff, 6
light from space, 26
liquid fuel/oxygen, 8
LM, 9, 10-11, 12
Lunar Roving Vehicle, 11

M

Manned Maneuvering Unit (MMU), 20, 21
Mars, 16, 17
Mercury spacecraft, 6
Meteosat, 23
Mission Control Center,

Houston, Texas, 12, 14, 18
MMU, 20, 21
modules on *Voskhod 2*, 7

N

NASA, 10, 12, 26

O

Orbiter (Shuttle), 18
orbiter (space probe), 16, 17

P

payloads, 23
pressure, 6, 20
pressure suits, 13
probes, 16, 24, 25
propellants, 8

R

radar, 11, 12
radio signals, 24, 26
reaction-control engines, 3
reentry, 6, 12, 19
remote-controlled arm, 16
Remote Manipulator System (RMS), 19
rescue ball, 21
RMS, 19
robot arm, 19
rocket boosters, 18, 22
rockets, 6, 8, 9, 11
    Ariane 4, 22-23
    Saturn V, 8-9, 10, 15

S

Salyut space station, 14
satellites, 6, 19, 22, 23, 26
Saturn V rocket, 8-9, 10, 15
Service Module (SM), 9, 10, 13
shower, 15
Shuttle, 18-19, 27

Skylab, 14-15
sleep station, 18
SM, 9, 10, 13
solar arrays, 15, 26
space buggy, 11
space race, 6
Space Shuttle, 18-19, 27
space sickness, 6
space suits, 7, 10, 13, 21
space telescope, 26
space walk, 7, 20-21
SPELDA, 23
Sputnik 1, 6
stages,
    Ariane 4, 22, 23
    Saturn V, 9

T

telescope mount, 15
tether, 7, 20
thrusters, on MMU, 21
tiles, heat-proof, 19

U

unmanned space probes, 16, 24, 25

V

Viking probes, 16-17
Voskhod 2, 7
Vostok spacecraft, 7
Voyager probes, 24

W

weightlessness, 6, 15, 18, 19

Acknowledgments

Dorling Kindersley would like to thank the following people who helped in the preparation of this book:

Lynn Bresler for the index
Additional artworks by Brihton Illustration